# Zion
## National Park

**by Mike Graf**

**Content Consultant:**
Ron Terry
Zion National Park
National Park Service

# Bridgestone Books

an imprint of Capstone Press
Mankato, Minnesota

Bridgestone Books are published by Capstone Press
151 Good Counsel Drive, P.O. Box 669, Mankato, Minnesota 56002
http://www.capstone-press.com

*Library of Congress Cataloging-in-Publication Data*
Graf, Mike.
  Zion National Park / by Mike Graf.
    v. cm.—(National parks)
    Contents: Zion National Park—How Zion formed—People in Zion—Animals—
Plants—Weather—Activities—Safety—Park issues—Map activity—About national parks—
Words to know.
    Includes bibliographical references (p. 23) and index.
    ISBN 0-7368-2222-4 (hardcover)
    1. Zion National Park (Utah)—Juvenile literature. [1. Zion National Park (Utah) 2.
National parks and reserves.]  I. Title. II. Series: National parks (Mankato, Minn.)
F832.Z8G73 2004
508.792'48—dc21                                                         2003000307

**Editorial Credits**

Heather Adamson, editor; Linda Clavel, series designer; Enoch Peterson, book designer;
  Anne McMullen, illustrator; Alta Schaffer, photo researcher; Karen Risch, product
  planning editor

**Photo Credits**

Bruce Coleman Inc./Larry Allan, 10
Eric Foltz Photography, 16
Houserstock, 18
Jeff Henry/Roche Jaune Pictures, Inc., 8, 14
John Elk III, cover, 4, 6, 12, 17
Tom Till, 1

1  2  3  4  5  6  08  07  06  05  04  03

# Table of Contents

Utah

# Zion National Park

Zion is home to steep cliffs, deep canyons, and strange rock formations. Zion's deep, winding Virgin River canyon is a highlight of the park. One of the largest natural arches in the world, Kolob Arch, rests in Zion.

Although Zion is in the desert, water runs through the park. Snow melts off Zion's mountains to form streams and rivers. The streams and rivers cut through the canyons. Ferns, flowers, and lush plants grow along the canyons.

Zion's canyons and cliffs also display the area's geology. Layers of rock sit uncovered and show off the history of the landscape.

In 1919, the government set aside land for Zion National Park. The park covers 229 square miles (593 square kilometers) in southwestern Utah. About 2.5 million people visit Zion each year.

**The Virgin River winds through Zion National Park.**

# How Zion Formed

Millions of years ago, the Zion area was flat. Layers of sand, mud, and gravel washed down from nearby mountains. These layers grew to be 10,000 feet (3,000 meters) thick.

Minerals soaked into Zion's layers. The minerals helped to turn the layers into stone. These minerals also give Zion's rocks their colors.

Over time, the ground shifted and stone was pushed up to form mountains. The height of the new mountains made streams run faster. These rushing streams started to erode, or wear away, the layers of rock. Deep canyons were formed by the running water. One of these streams, the Virgin River, carved beautiful Zion Canyon. The river is still eroding the canyon today. Zion Canyon forms the main area of Zion National Park.

**Different minerals make the many colors of rock. Layers of sandstone formed into Zion's mountains.**

8

# People in Zion

American Indians have lived in the Zion area for many years. About 2,000 years ago, Anasazi, or ancestral puebloans, lived in Zion. Art, tools, and baskets of the Anasazi have been found in the park. The Kaibab Band of Paiute Indians hunted and lived in Zion Canyon for hundreds of years.

Around the 1840s, Brigham Young and his Mormon followers settled in Utah. They were the first European Americans in the area. Mormon Nephite Johnson is believed to be the first European to discover Zion.

Leo A. Snow explored Zion Canyon in 1908. He thought the area was beautiful. He convinced President Howard Taft to make it Mukuntuweap National Monument. Mukuntuweap was the Paiute name for the area. But local settlers called the area Zion, which means "a peaceful place." In 1918 and 1919, the government made the park larger. Its name was also changed to Zion National Park.

**Rock art carved by American Indians about 2,000 years ago can still be seen in Zion National Park.**

# Animals

Songs of tree frogs often greet spring visitors to Zion Park. Tree frogs are one of the many creatures that make the park their home. Snakes and lizards can be seen slithering and scrambling along the ground. The desert tortoise and Gila monster also live near Zion.

Zion's mountains and canyons provide a home for large animals. Coyotes, mountain lions, and bobcats prowl through the canyons. Bighorn sheep roam the canyons and steep rock areas. Elk and a few black bear live high in the mountains.

Smaller animals like foxes, weasels, and skunks also live throughout the park. Raccoons roam the lower Zion Valley. Bats search the night sky for insects.

Many kinds of birds live in Zion. Golden eagles circle the park's skies. Canyon wrens fly around the cliffs and rocks.

Coyotes in Zion's mountains howl, yip, and bark to signal each other.

# Plants

Zion Canyon has many plants. Ferns, mosses, and wildflowers cling to wet cliffs. They form the "hanging gardens." The plants grow out from small cracks in the cliffs and hang over the rock.

Zion Canyon also contains many large trees. Oaks, maples, cottonwoods, and birch trees are common in the canyon. Thick forests of ponderosa pines grow in Zion's higher mountains. The leaves of aspen trees in Zion change colors in the fall.

Plants in some parts of Zion get little water. Desert plants live in these areas. Desert plants save water inside thick skins or long, shallow roots. Some of Zion's desert plants include yucca and prickly pear cactus.

The prickly pear cactus and many other desert plants grow in areas of the park that receive little water.

# Weather

Each season at Zion gives visitors a different experience. As weather changes with each season, so do the activities in the park.

Spring brings mild temperatures. Hikers can watch the wildflowers start to bloom.

Most visitors come to Zion in summer. Temperatures can soar to more than 100 degrees Fahrenheit (38 degrees Celsius) during the day. Visitors stay cool by hiking in shady canyons. Thunderstorms often occur in summer.

Fall at Zion is usually clear and cool. The weather begins to get colder in late fall. Visitors can see leaves turning color. Zion's mountains may get a layer of snow.

Winters in Zion Canyon are cool and may bring snow. Most of the snow falls in the mountains. Temperatures in winter can be below freezing. They can also be as high as 60 degrees Fahrenheit (16 degrees Celsius).

**Snow falls in the park during winter. Most snow occurs in the mountains, but sometimes it falls in the canyons too.**

# Activities

Zion National Park is a hiker's park. The park's 120 miles (193 kilometers) of trails offer short canyon walks or steep cliff climbs. The Weeping Rock Trail passes a cliff that drips with water. It appears to be crying. The Narrows Trail has cliffs on either side that stand up to 2,000 feet (600 meters) high. Angels Landing leads to a view of Zion Canyon.

People can also ride horses or bicycles along a few paths in the park. Experienced climbers can get permits to scale Zion's rock faces.

# Safety

It is important to be safe while exploring Zion. Hikers should drink plenty of water and wear proper shoes.

Many of Zion's trails are next to steep cliffs. Hikers must pay attention to where they step so they do not fall.

Summer thunderstorms can cause the Virgin River to flood suddenly. Visitors should check weather reports before hiking the park's trails.

# Park Issues

For many years, overcrowding was an issue at Zion National Park. The small park gets lots of visitors. Most visit Zion Canyon. Many canyon parking lots and roads were too full. To reduce crowding, visitors now ride buses into the park.

Crowding is still a challenge on some of Zion's hiking trails. The many hikers have damaged trails. More workers are needed to keep the trails safe.

People also create problems by feeding deer in the campgrounds. These deer get used to being fed and do not learn to find food for themselves. Deer also lose their fear of people when they are fed. These deer sometimes injure people who get too close to them. When this happens, the deer must be killed.

Park workers teach visitors about the park's wildlife and plants. The more people know about the park, the better they are able to take care of it. Then, people can enjoy Zion National Park for many years.

**Visitors load a bus heading for Zion Canyon. Buses reduce crowding on canyon roads and parking lots.**

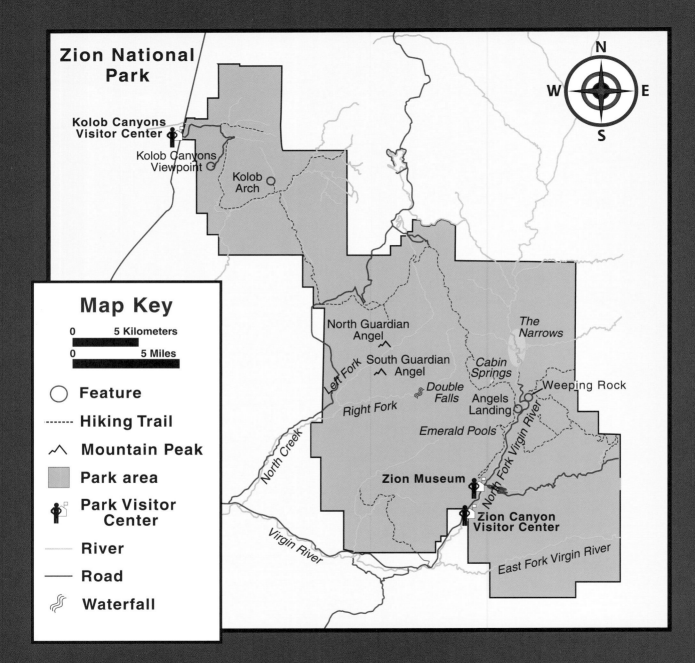

# Map Activity

Zion's visitors use hiking trails to explore places like Angels Landing, Kolob Arch, the Narrows, Weeping Rock, and Emerald Pools. See if you can figure out how far it is from one feature to the next using the map and scale.

**What You Need**

String

**What You Do**

1. Find a visitor center on the map. Pretend you are going hiking. Pick one of Zion's features to visit.
2. Measure the distance along the hiking trails between the visitor center and the feature you picked. Lay string along the path. Use the map's scale to figure out how far the distance is between the two.
3. Pick a few other places to visit and do the same thing. Figure out how far you must travel from the visitor center to the feature you picked. Or measure from one feature to the next feature.

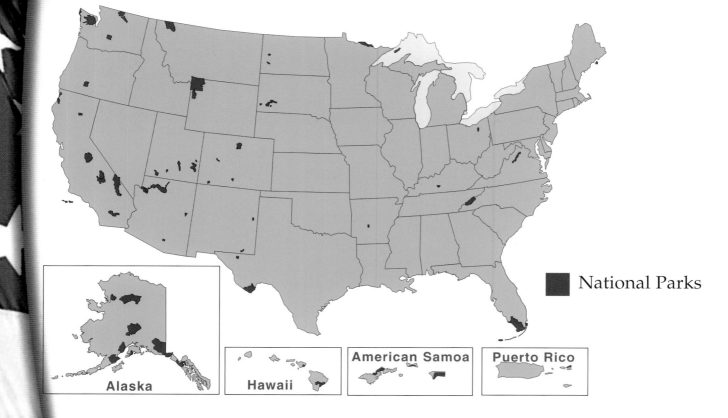

National Parks

Alaska

Hawaii

American Samoa

Puerto Rico

## About National Parks

The U.S. government creates national parks to protect special natural areas. These parks allow everyone to enjoy the beauty of a place such as Zion. People can camp, hike, and view scenery in national parks. But they are not allowed to hunt or build on park lands. Today, the United States has more than 50 national parks.

# Words to Know

**arch** (ARCH)—a curved, open formation in rock

**canyon** (KAN-yuhn)—a deep, narrow area with steep sides

**desert** (DEZ-urt)—a very dry area of land

**erosion** (ee-ROH-zhuhn)—the wearing away of land by water or wind

**mineral** (MIN-ur-uhl)—a substance found in nature that is not made by a plant or animal; minerals can be found on Earth's surface or underground.

**Mormon** (MOR-muhn)—a member of The Church of Jesus Christ of Latter-day Saints

# Read More

**Petersen, David.** *National Parks.* A True Book. New York: Children's Press, 2001.

**Raatma, Lucia.** *Our National Parks.* Let's See. Minneapolis: Compass Point Books, 2002.

# Useful Addresses

**National Park Service**
1849 C Street NW
Washington, DC  20240

**Zion National Park**
SR9
Springdale, Utah  84767

# Internet Sites

Do you want to find out more about Zion National Park?
Let FactHound, our fact-finding hound dog,
do the research for you.

**Here's how:**
1) Visit *www.facthound.com*
2) Type in the **Book ID** number: **0736822224**
3) Click on **FETCH IT**.

FactHound will fetch Internet sites picked by our editors
just for you!

# Index